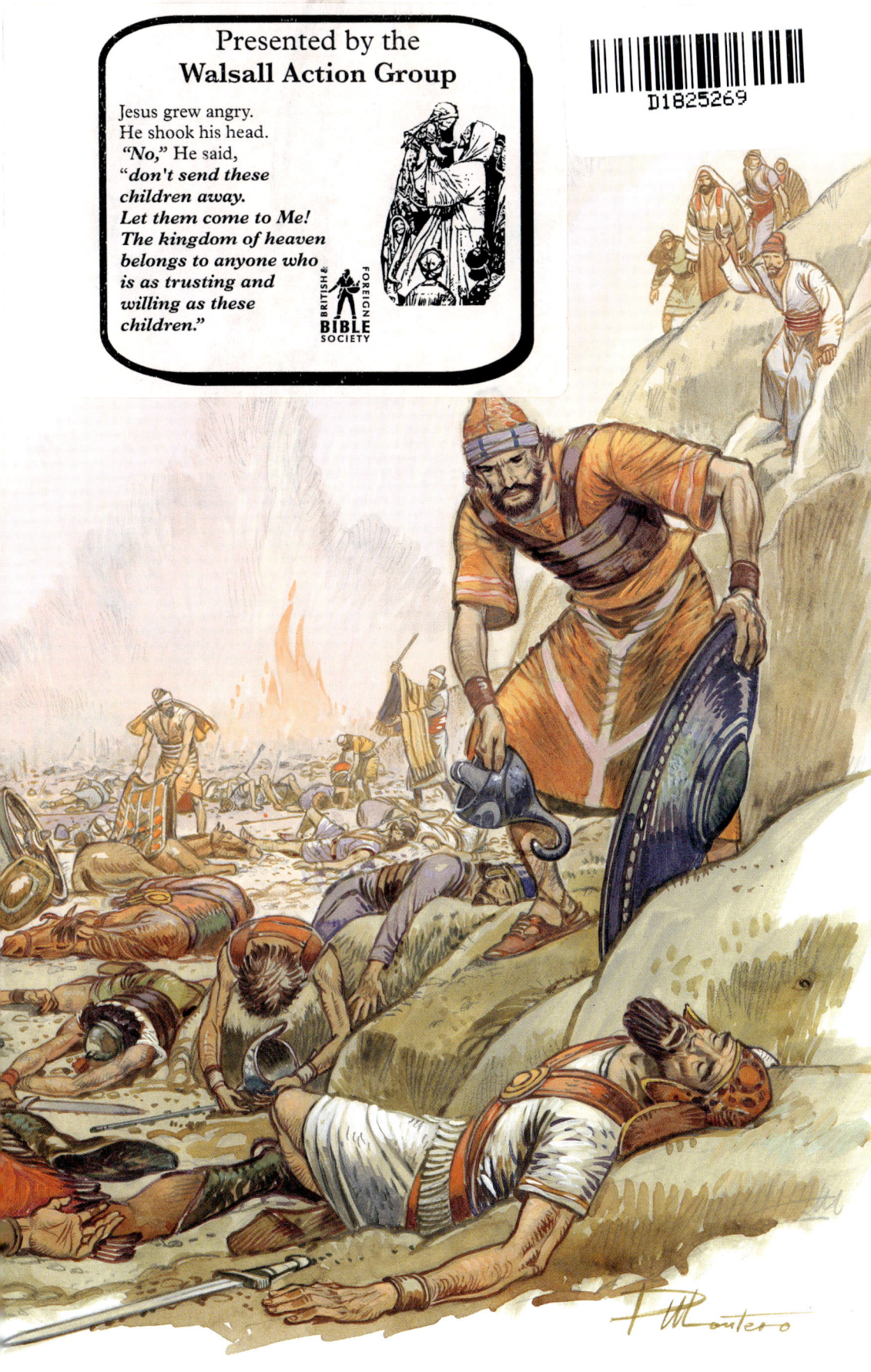

D1825269

Adventure Story Bible
Book 12

Working Wonders

Written by Anne de Graaf

Illustrated by José Pérez Montero

Bible Society

Working Wonders

Contents – 1 Kings 13–19, 21–22; 2 Kings 1–2, 9, 17, 22; 2 Chronicles 12–14, 17–20

Book 12 – Bible background   3

TROUBLE IN ISRAEL
A visit from the man of God   4
Jeroboam's punishment   5
Rehoboam's reign in Judah   6
Kings of Israel and Judah   8
Evil Queen Jezebel   9

ONE OF THE GREATEST PROPHETS
The birds feed the prophet   10
Endless food   11
The widow's son comes back to life   12
Elijah meets the king   13
The contest   14
Fire and rain   16

ELIJAH SPEAKS IN THE NAME OF GOD
Elijah has a hard time   18
A gentle whisper   18
God gives Elijah a helper   20
Ahab wants a bigger garden   22
The king gets what he wants   24

ISRAEL AND JUDAH
Many false prophets and one real one . . .   24
The story of Jehoshaphat   26
The last days of Elijah   28
The chariot of fire   29

Other Adventure Story Bible titles   32

Book 12 — Bible background

Following the reign of King Solomon the one Israelite nation had split into two parts — Israel in the north and Judah in the south. It was one of the darkest times in the history of God's people. Most of the kings were very bad and they often led the people into doing evil things. This was the time for Elijah and Elisha to bring God's message to the people.

Elijah was one of the greatest prophets. Time after time he worked miracles to show the people that the God of Israel was the true God, and that they should stop worshipping false gods. They should put the one, true God first, loving him more than anyone else.

When the people refused to do this, the entire nation suffered as a result. The poor became poorer, and the leaders cheated and lied to the people.

The people of Israel believed that when their expected Messiah came, Elijah would return to earth.

Elisha was chosen by God to take Elijah's place. Elisha worked more miracles than any other prophet. He was also very brave, and always knew that God was helping him.

Elijah and Elisha had similar names and similar work. The work which God gave them was to warn the people of Israel that they must stop disobeying God. Otherwise they would be punished, captured by their enemies, and taken away from their homeland.

TROUBLE IN ISRAEL

A visit from the man of God

1 Kings 13.1-10, 33-34

After the reign of King Solomon the nation of God's people had split into two kingdoms, Judah in the south and Israel in the north. They were divided because the people and their kings had disobeyed God and chosen to worship other gods. God had given his people laws to prevent them from doing such wrong things, and to help them live good lives. Now that hardly anyone paid attention to these laws, many people were suffering because of their leaders' selfishness and greed. People who were poor, ill, or widowed, found that no one protected them any more. Many of the priests were also bad.

There were two kings for the divided kingdom. Rehoboam, king of Judah, was the son of Solomon. His throne was in the holy city, Jerusalem, and during his early years as king he did his best to put God's laws into practice in every way. The poor were cared for and there was justice and peace in the land. All the Lord's priests were in Jerusalem, where the people still obeyed God.

But the other king, Jeroboam of Israel, was evil. He worshipped other gods and led the people away from the Lord. He built altars and places of worship which were not in honour of the God of Israel.

One day, when King Jeroboam was worshipping at one of the altars he had made at Bethel, a prophet of God went up to him and said, "You are very wrong to worship these other gods! A child called Josiah will be born into David's family, and he will put a stop to this. As a sign that what I say comes from the Lord, this altar will fall apart, and the ashes on it will be scattered."

King Jeroboam did not like what the prophet said. He shook his fist at him and shouted in anger, "Seize him!" As soon as he

4

did that, the king's arm became paralyzed, and he couldn't move it. At the same time there was a loud rumble and the altar fell apart. This was a sign and a warning to the people of Israel that they should do what the prophet said, and stop worshipping other gods.

King Jeroboam cried out to the prophet, "Please, speak to the Lord for me and ask him to make my arm better."

So the prophet prayed, and the king's arm became as it was before. Then the king invited the prophet to come to the palace for something to eat. He also tried to buy the favour of the prophet by giving him a gift.

But the prophet answered the king, "Even if you were to give me half of all you own, I would not go with you, or eat or drink with you. The Lord told me not to eat or drink, and not to return home by the way I came." Then he turned and went home a different way, obeying what the Lord had told him.

But King Jeroboam ignored the warning and continued worshipping other gods. This was asking for trouble. God had warned Jeroboam to stop, and would punish him for disobeying his rules.

Jeroboam's punishment

1 Kings 14.1–20; 2 Kings 17.6

At that time King Jeroboam's son fell ill. Jeroboam told his wife to go and see the prophet Ahijah and ask if the boy would get better.

Ahijah was the prophet who, many years earlier, had told Jeroboam he would one day become king of Israel.

Jeroboam said to his wife, "Disguise yourself when you go to see Ahijah, so that no one will recognize you. Take him gifts of bread, cakes, and honey."

When Jeroboam's wife went to ask Ahijah about her son, she covered her face and pretended she wasn't the king's wife.

Ahijah was a very old man and had become blind, but God was with him. The Lord said

5

that her husband was more blind than Ahijah. The king had refused to see what God wanted him to do and now it was too late.

Ahijah told her that God would tear the kingdom away from Jeroboam. God was angry and would bring disaster on Jeroboam and his family. When his wife went home the sick boy would die.

The prophet said that the people would also be punished for turning away from God. God would let Israel be defeated, and he would take their land away from them. "The Lord will scatter the Israelites," Ahijah said, "to lands beyond the River Eupharates."

Many years later this did indeed happen. When the king of Assyria conquered the Israelites, the people were sent to those far-off lands.

When Jeroboam's wife returned home, she was very upset. The moment she entered her house, her boy died. In time, all of Jeroboam's family were murdered. Everything happened just as the prophet of God had said it would.

Rehoboam's reign in Judah

1 Kings 14.21–31; 2 Chronicles 12.1–12
Jeroboam began and ended his reign in a bad way, disobeying the Lord. But the other king, Rehoboam of Judah, at least began his rule in the right way. When he became king, Rehoboam invited all those who worshipped the one, true God to come to Jerusalem, God's chosen city. But as the years passed, even Rehoboam chose to disobey God.

The people in Jerusalem turned away from the Lord and did terrible things. They committed the worst sins ever practised by any of God's chosen people. They built places of worship for false gods, and put up statues and pillars on hills, worshipping them instead of the Lord. These things became more important to them than God. Because of this God took his protection away from Judah, and the country went from bad to worse.

Because the people and the king were bad,

to him, "Jeroboam's wife is coming to ask you whether or not their child will die. She will pretend to be someone else."

Later, when Ahijah heard Jeroboam's wife step into his house, he said, "Come in, wife of Jeroboam. Why do you pretend to be another woman? I have bad news from the Lord for you."

The wife of Jeroboam didn't know what to think. She was scared by this blind man who knew who she was, and as she listened to his message she became even more frightened. The more she heard, the more she realized the nation became weak. God let this happen because the people had broken their promises.

It did not take long for the king of Egypt to see what was happening and take his opportunity. He attacked Jerusalem with more than one thousand chariots and tens of thousands of horsemen. There were more soldiers than could be counted. On his way, the king of Egypt captured many cities of Judah.

When his army was at the gates of Jerusalem, a prophet came to King Rehoboam. He said, "The Lord says, 'Because you have left me, I will now leave you.' " Rehoboam knew he was in trouble. He was afraid of being killed by the Egyptians. Rehoboam and all the leaders of the people realized what they had done, and were sorry. "The Lord is acting fairly against us," they said.

So the Lord said through the prophet, "Because they feel sorry for what they have done, I will not let them be destroyed. I will rescue them, but the Egyptians will still capture Jerusalem. That way you will learn the difference between serving me and serving the kings of other lands. I will protect my people and they will not be killed."

The Lord used this as a lesson to Judah. Because the people were so stubborn, they needed to learn the hard way. But God is always willing to forgive and to listen when people turn to him.

When Egypt attacked Jerusalem, the people of Judah were not able to defeat the Egyptians. The king of Egypt and his soldiers stole the treasure out of Solomon's beautiful temple for the Lord, as well as from the royal palace. The Egyptians took everything, even all the shields of gold which Solomon had made. But they did not take the people with them. The people were kept safe, just as the Lord had promised.

Kings of Israel and Judah

1 Kings 15.1—16.28; 2 Chronicles 13.1—14.15

After King Rehoboam of Judah died, his son
Abijah took his place. When the Egyptians
had attacked Jerusalem Rehoboam had said
he was sorry for disobeying God, but later he
went back to his bad ways. Now his son was
no better.

But the Lord still would not destroy
Rehoboam's family. This was because God
had promised King David that his family
would always sit on the throne, and
Rehoboam came from King David's family.
David had wanted to do what God asked of
him, and he worshipped only the Lord. When
David had disobeyed God he had said he was
sorry, and meant it.

When Rehoboam's son died, Rehoboam's
grandson took the throne. He was called Asa,
and was a good king who wanted more than
anything else to please God. He commanded
the people of Judah to seek the God of their
fathers and to obey the rules which God had
given Moses. King Asa ruled for forty-one
years, and under him Jerusalem once again
became the city of God, a place where his
chosen people could come and worship.

But while Asa was king he had to fight wars
against the other kingdom, Israel. In order to
fight these wars King Asa made an alliance
with neighbouring Assyria. To do this he
stripped what was left of all the silver and gold
from the temple of God and paid Assyria to
help fight against Israel.

Asa also led thousands of Judah's best
fighting men in a battle against the Sudanese.
All these were brave fighting men, but the
Sudanese had more soldiers than Asa's army.

Asa called out to God, "Lord, you can help
a weak army as easily as a powerful one. We
trust in you and fight today in your name!"

After Asa's prayer, God gave the soldiers of
Judah a mighty victory that day. The Lord
listened to King Asa because he trusted God
and obeyed him.

Evil Queen Jezebel

1 Kings 16.29–33

During the years when Asa was king of Judah, Israel had one bad king after another. Time after time people killed each other, fought, or plotted against each other. The nation of Israel was very bad.

Of all the evil kings who ruled over Israel during the years that King Asa ruled over Judah, one was worse than the rest. His name was Ahab. Ahab thought that the rules that God had given them did not matter.

Ahab married a woman named Jezebel. She was not an Israelite, but a princess from Sidon, a foreign tribe. Ahab should not have married her, because Jezebel's people did not worship the Lord. Through living with her Ahab went further and further away from God. Jezebel tried to kill the prophets of the Lord, and to make the people worship her gods instead. So Ahab built an altar honouring Baal, and made the people worship him. He also put up a statue of the goddess Asherah to be worshipped, and the people did what their king told them.

During the twenty-two years that Ahab ruled as king, the people of Israel became worse than they ever had been.

ONE OF THE GREATEST PROPHETS
The birds feed the prophet

1 Kings 17.1-7

It was during this very dark time in Israel's history that God sent one of his greatest prophets, Elijah. He was to bring God's word to the people and warn them to turn back to God.

Elijah went to King Ahab and said, "As surely as the Lord, the God of Israel lives, not one more drop of rain or dew will fall until I ask him for it!"

Then the Lord told Elijah to go and hide near a brook east of the Jordan. Elijah had given his warning to the king, and now he would wait until the Lord told him what to do next.

While Elijah was living near this brook, the Lord took care of Elijah in an amazing way. He commanded ravens to bring Elijah bread and meat every morning and evening, and Elijah had plenty of water to drink from the brook.

But after a while the brook dried up because there was no rain. It was not the only place without water. The whole of Israel was as dry as a desert, and the crops could not grow. The animals were so thirsty they died, and the people were thirsty, too. Even King Ahab and Queen Jezebel didn't have enough to drink. The Lord was trying to teach the people of Israel that he was the living God, the only true God.

Endless food

1 Kings 17.7–16

When the brook dried up Elijah had no more water, and the Lord told him to go to a village near Sidon. This was Jezebel's home country, where many people worshipped Baal.

"Go at once to this place and stay there," the Lord said. I will make sure that a widow there will give you food."

Elijah did as God told him, and saw a widow gathering firewood at the gate of the city. He could see she was very poor. Her clothes were wearing out, and she hadn't been eating much for a long time.

"Please," he asked her, "could you get me a little water in a jar, so I could have a drink?"

As she was going to get it he asked, "Please might I have some bread, as well?"

The woman shook her head. "I have no bread," she said. "In fact, this firewood I gathered is for a fire to cook my last meal. My son and I have nothing left but a handful of flour and a little oil in the jar. I was going to make our last loaf from that, then lie down to die."

Elijah said to the woman, "Don't be afraid. Make the food for you and your son, but first make a small loaf for me.

"The Lord God of Israel says, 'Your bowl of flour and jar of oil will not run out until the day that the Lord sends rain.' "

So the widow did as Elijah said, and a miracle took place! Every time she made a loaf for her son or for Elijah it looked as though the flour and oil were just about to run out. Then the next day there was still enough for one more meal.

"Look! It's a miracle!" she called to her son. She held out the loaf, shaking her head in wonder.

"How can that be?" her son said. "I thought you said you used up the last of the flour and oil yesterday."

"I know," she said, "but every day there is still enough!" In this way the widow and her son always had enough to eat, and the Lord supplied food for Elijah. Elijah came to live with the widow and she took care of him, feeding him and giving him a place to sleep.

The widow's son comes back to life

1 Kings 17.17–24

While Elijah was staying with the widow her son became very ill. Each day the boy grew weaker, and finally he died.

This boy was the only relative the woman had. Her husband was dead, and without her son she had no one to take care of her in her old age. There wouldn't be anybody to earn money or work in the fields, and she would have to beg for food. Her son meant everything to her, and she could think of nothing but her sadness.

So the widow turned against Elijah. "Why do I have anything to do with you?" she said. "If you're such a great man of God, why am I being punished now? Look, my son is dead!"

"Give him to me," Elijah said. He took the boy from the woman's arms and carried him upstairs to his own room. He laid the boy on his bed and prayed.

"O Lord, my God, why have you brought such sadness on this widow? She has taken care of me. Why did you cause her son to ie?" Then he stretched himself out on the child's body. He did this three times and prayed, "Oh Lord my God, please put life back into this child's body!"

The Lord heard Elijah's prayer. The boy took one deep breath and his body shook. After a pause, he took another breath, then another. In a few moments his eyes fluttered open. He had come back from the dead! Elijah brought the boy downstairs to his mother. "Look, your son is alive!" he said.

The woman cried out in surprise. Tears streamed down her face as she hugged her son, and the boy smiled at his mother.

"Now I know that you are a man of God," she told Elijah, "and that whatever you say in the Lord's name is true. There can be no doubt that the Lord has blessed you!"

Elijah meets the king

1 Kings 18.1–19

Elijah stayed a long time with the woman and her son. For three years there had been no rain in the land. All the rivers and streams had dried up, and most of the wells. Animals were dying, and people went hungry and thirsty.

During this time King Ahab had been looking everywhere for Elijah. He remembered that Elijah had said rain would fall only when Elijah prayed for it, so Ahab had sent soldiers out in every direction to find the prophet. But no one could find him. No one knew that he was hiding near Sidon in the house of a widow and her son.

While Ahab had been looking for Elijah, Queen Jezebel had ordered that all the Lord's priests should be killed. She didn't want them to worship their God, who had stopped the rain from falling. But an important man called Obadiah, who was in charge of the palace, managed to hide one hundred prophets in two caves, and was even able to find food and water for them.

One day, Obadiah went looking for water for the king's cattle, horses, and mules. As he searched, who should he find walking towards him but Elijah! "Is it really you, Elijah?" he cried out.

"Yes," Elijah said. "Go and tell the king that I am here."

But Obadiah was afraid. The king had searched everywhere for Elijah and made everyone swear that they didn't know where he was. "If I tell the king I have found you, he'll have me killed! Besides, you might disappear again," Obadiah said.

But Elijah told him not to be afraid, he would meet the king that very day. When Obadiah told King Ahab where Elijah was, Ahab hurried to meet him.

"Is that really you, you troublemaker of Israel?" he called to Elijah.

"I am not a troublemaker," Elijah said. "You and your family are the ones who have caused so much trouble because you chose to follow Baal instead of God. This is his way of showing you who the true God really is. Now bring the four hundred and fifty prophets of Baal and the four hundred prophets of Asherah, the goddess your Queen Jezebel supports. Then we will see whose god is real!"

The contest

1 Kings 18.20–36

The time had come for God to work a miracle so great that his people could no longer doubt that he was the true God. For the last three years the people had heard their king and queen say, "Worship Baal. Baal will look after you. Just wait and see."

But even though the people sacrificed to Baal, he didn't answer them. That was because Baal was not God. Only the Lord God could answer their prayers. Now he wanted to show the people through Elijah that he was the only God they should worship.

After three years without rain, God sent Elijah to challenge the king and people of Israel to a contest. Elijah went up to Mount Carmel. There he waited for the king to bring the many hundreds of prophets of Baal.

All the people gathered around the mountain. Elijah called out to the crowd, "How much longer will it take you to make up your minds? You can't worship God and Baal! Make a choice between the two. If the Lord is God, then follow him! But if Baal is god, follow him!"

The people said nothing. They waited and watched. Then Elijah said, "I am the only prophet who stands here in the name of the Lord, but Baal has hundreds and hundreds of prophets. Now bring us two bulls."

Elijah told the priests of Baal to kill their bull and lay it on the wood, but not to light a fire under it. He would do the same with his bull and wood. "Call on your god to light a fire under the bull, and I will call on my God! The God who answers with fire is the real God."

All the people agreed that this was a very fair test. The priests of Baal prayed from morning until noon, "O Baal, answer us." But there was no answer. They danced and shouted louder and louder, jumping around the altar. But still there was no answer. No fire burnt the wood beneath their bull.

Elijah made fun of them and said, "Call again. Maybe your god is busy, or he's gone on a journey. Or maybe he is asleep and needs to be woken up!"

So they cried out again and even cut themselves, as was their custom, so that blood dripped from their arms. But still their god did not answer. In the end they were worn out from dancing and shouting, but nothing happened. No one answered.

Then it was Elijah's turn. He set about repairing the altar of the Lord which had been destroyed. He took twelve stones for the twelve tribes of Israel and rebuilt the altar with them. Then he put the wood and the bull onto it. Four large jars of water were poured over the altar three times, until the trench which ran round the altar was full. Then Elijah the prophet started praying.

Fire and rain

1 Kings 18.37–46

Elijah lifted his hands up towards heaven. He prayed calmly and slowly, so that everyone could hear. "O Lord, the God of Abraham, Isaac, and Jacob, let it be known today that you are God and I am your servant. Answer me, Lord, so that these people may know that you are the Lord. Show us that you are the living God and the true God of Israel who will bring them back to you."

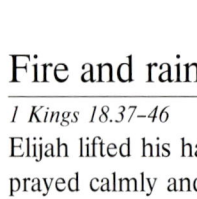

Suddenly the Lord sent fire! The wood, the stones, the earth, and the bull were all burnt up in the fire. The heat was terrible.

"Look! The Lord has sent fire!" the crowds shouted. Then all the people bowed down to the ground together shouting, "The Lord, he is God!"

Then Elijah told the people, "Seize the priests of Baal, and don't let any of them get away!" So the people did as he said, and Elijah killed them.

Then Elijah turned to King Ahab. "Go and eat," he said, "for I hear the roar of thunder."

While Ahab went to eat, Elijah crouched down on the earth and put his face between his knees. Now that the people of Israel had said they believed the Lord was God, Elijah hoped that God would let rain fall on the land.

He told his servant to watch the sky over the sea, and look for clouds. At first there was nothing. Time after time Elijah told his servant to go and look. The seventh time, the servant said, "Look! There's a cloud the size of a man's hand. It's coming up from the sea!"

Elijah sent his servant to Ahab with the news. "Get your chariot and go back home before the rain stops you."

Within moments the sky grew black with clouds, the wind blew, and the rain poured down. The people raised their hands and cheered. After three years of drought, they now had rain!

The power of the Lord came on Elijah, so that he ran faster than the horses pulling King Ahab's chariot, and faster than the wind. Elijah ran so fast, he arrived home before the king did!

ELIJAH SPEAKS IN THE NAME OF GOD

Elijah has a hard time

1 Kings 19.1–8

When Elijah arrived in the king's city of Jezreel, he took shelter from the rain, and waited. "Will King Ahab and the people turn from their evil ways now?" he wondered. "After seeing God's miracle, will they worship the one true God?"

It didn't take long for Elijah to find out. When King Ahab arrived in Jezreel, he went straight to Queen Jezebel. "Something strange and terrible has happened!" he said. He told her how Elijah had called on his God and brought down both fire and rain. Jezebel was angry, and when she heard that Elijah had killed the priests of Baal, Jezebel turned purple with rage.

"How dare he do this?" she screamed. She sent a message to Elijah. She threatened, "May the gods kill me, too, if I have not killed you by this time tomorrow!"

It was a terrible message. Elijah shivered when he heard her threat, and ran for his life.

He went off into the wilderness by himself, and stopped to rest under a tree. There he slid down onto the ground. In the shade of the tree he prayed, "I've had enough, Lord. I just can't take any more. I might as well be dead."

Elijah was very miserable. He felt so tired that he lay down and went to sleep. Suddenly Elijah felt something touch his shoulder. An angel of the Lord was beside him and said, "Get up Elijah, and have something to eat and drink."

Elijah looked round and saw a loaf of bread and a jar of water which had appeared right next to him. He sat up and ate and drank, then lay down again.

Then the angel of the Lord came a second time and touched Elijah. "Get up and eat some more. You have to make a long journey and you need strength for it."

So Elijah did as the angel told him. The rest and the food did him good, and Elijah didn't feel so sad. Feeling much stronger, he went further into the wilderness. He travelled for forty days and forty nights until he reached Mount Sinai, the mountain on which God had given Moses the Ten Commandments so many years before.

A gentle whisper

1 Kings 19.9–18

When Elijah reached Mount Sinai he went into a cave and fell asleep there. It had been a very long journey. Suddenly he heard the voice of the Lord ask him, "What are you doing here, Elijah?"

"Lord, I have always served you — you alone," Elijah answered. "But your chosen people have forgotten about you. They have torn down your altars and killed your prophets. I'm the only one left. I am all alone. And now they want to kill me, too!"

Despite the miracle of fire and rain which God had worked through Elijah, Elijah had lost all hope and was very sad.

The Lord said, "Get up, and go and stand on the mountain before the Lord." An incredible thing was about to happen. The Lord himself would pass by Elijah!

All at once a ferocious wind tore through the mountains and split the rocks apart. But the Lord was not in the wind. After the wind an earthquake shook the land, but the Lord was not in the earthquake.

After the earthquake a fire burnt everything for miles around. But the Lord was not in the fire. Elijah waited at the mouth of the cave.

Then there came the sound of a gentle whisper. Elijah heard it and looked up. He covered his face with his cloak and went out and stood at the entrance to the cave.

A voice said, "What are you doing here, Elijah?"

Elijah sighed and said again, "Lord, I have always served you — you alone. But your chosen people have forgotten about you. They have torn down your altars and killed your prophets. I'm the only one left. I am all alone. And now they want to kill me, too!" Elijah felt sorry for himself, and he was afraid. He thought his life was almost over.

But the Lord told him, "Go back into the wilderness, then enter the city of Damascus. There you will anoint new kings over Assyria and Israel. You will anoint Elisha, too, to be your helper and to become prophet in your place."

God knew how Elijah felt. It was a hard thing for Elijah to try and turn the people back to God on his own. Elijah needed a friend and helper. Elisha would be that person.

"And Elijah," the Lord continued. "You are not really the only one left worshipping me. There are seven thousand people in Israel who have not bowed down to Baal and worshipped him."

Elijah felt much better now and smiled. "Thank you, Lord," he said. "Things aren't as bad as I thought they were."

God gives Elijah a helper

1 Kings 19.19–21

Elijah came out of the wilderness feeling much better than when he went into it. He was ready to go and do whatever the Lord asked of him.

He went to find Elisha. Elisha was ploughing a field with a team of oxen. Elijah came up to him and took off his cloak, putting it on Elisha's shoulders. This told Elisha that he had been called to follow and learn from Elijah. Elisha knew what it meant.

He left his oxen and ran after Elijah. "Please sir!" he called out. "Let me kiss my father and my mother good–bye, then I will follow you." Elijah agreed.

So Elisha killed the oxen with which he had been ploughing, and cooked them on a fire made with the yoke which had held the oxen together. Then Elisha passed some of the meat around to all the people there, including his family.

After saying good-bye to everyone, Elisha got up and followed Elijah. In the years to come Elisha would serve and help the great prophet. He would watch and learn from Elijah until it was his turn to take over as prophet for the Lord.

Elisha would carry on the work of bringing the people of Israel back to worshipping the Lord, and to lead them away from worshipping false gods.

Ahab wants a bigger garden

1 Kings 21.1-16

As the years went by, Elijah and Elisha
travelled throughout the land, preaching to the
people. But the evil Queen Jezebel had a
strong hold on the king and his people,
making them worship Baal, instead of the
Lord.

By this time King Ahab had become very
rich and powerful. He was often like a spoilt
child – if he saw something he liked, he
wanted it immediately. Jezebel, however, was
often much craftier than her husband.

Once King Ahab wanted a vineyard which
was in a place called Jezreel, next to his
palace. He went to the owner of the vineyard,
a man called Naboth.

"Give me your vineyard, so that I can make
it into a vegetable garden. If you agree, I'll
give you a better vineyard, or pay you for the
land."

But Naboth said, "I could never give away
the land my father gave to me. This land
belonged to my family before me and should
belong to us for ever."

King Ahab went away to the palace and
sulked like a little boy. He would not eat his
food. He was in his bedroom, lying on his

bed, when Queen Jezebel came to him and asked what was the matter.

"Naboth won't sell me his vineyard. I wanted the land for a vegetable garden! Now I can't have it," Ahab said.

Jezebel laughed. "What's the matter with you? That's no way for a king to behave! You can do whatever you want! You're the king, Ahab. Get up and have something to eat. Don't worry! I'll make sure you get Naboth's vineyard."

Jezebel worked out a plan to get rid of Naboth and all his family so that Ahab could have that piece of land. She wrote letters and signed Ahab's name on them. She called a

special meeting of the leaders of the city, including Naboth. Then she told two bad men to tell lies about Naboth at the meeting. While Naboth sat before all the men of the city, these two men made up terrible stories about him. "Naboth cursed God," they said, "and said bad things about the king."

"No!" Naboth cried. "It's a lie!" But no one believed him, since not just one, but two men had said he had cursed God and the king.

The men of the city stood up and seized Naboth. They dragged him outside the city gates and threw stones at him until he died.

When Queen Jezebel went to the king, she smiled wickedly. "Now you can have the vineyard you wanted, the one which belonged to Naboth, and make a garden of it. I've taken care of Naboth. He won't be in your way any more," she said.

The king gets what he wants

1 Kings 21.17–29; 22.37; 2 Kings 9.30–37

King Ahab went down to the vineyard which had belonged to Naboth and his family. Thanks to the lies arranged by his evil wife, Ahab now had what he wanted. He was all ready to take the land as his own, when suddenly Elijah appeared.

God had seen what had happened, and had sent Elijah to talk to the king. As soon as Ahab saw Elijah, he trembled with fear. "What do you want this time, my old enemy?

Elijah said, "The Lord wants you to know that he has seen you murder so you could steal this land. The Lord says that you and your family will die, and the dogs will lick your blood."

"Jezebel will be eaten by dogs," Elijah added, "here, near her own palace. That is the Lord's punishment."

There was never a king quite as evil as Ahab. He and his wicked wife Jezebel had done terrible deeds against the Lord. Soon they would know that they shouldn't have done these things.

When Ahab heard all this, he tore his clothes and begged for forgiveness. "I'm so sorry, please forgive me, Lord!" he cried.

During the next few weeks Ahab did not wear his fine clothes or eat good food, to show how sorry he was. So God told Elijah, "Because Ahab has humbled himself, I will not bring disaster on his family until after he is dead." All that Elijah had said would happen later came true.

ISRAEL AND JUDAH

Many false prophets and one real one

1 Kings 22.1–40; 2 Chronicles 18.1–34

After many years of wars between the two kingdoms of Judah and Israel they agreed to stop fighting. King Jehoshaphat of Judah had big walled cities and a very powerful army. He was also very rich and his throne was in Jerusalem. He arranged that his son would marry King Ahab's daughter. That way the two kingdoms could be friends instead of enemies.

But Jehoshaphat was not like King Ahab. He was a good king who tried to do what God asked him. Jehoshaphat went to visit Ahab and Ahab asked him to help him fight a war against Syria.

Jehoshaphat was not sure if he should go with Ahab or not. "Call the prophets and ask them whether or not we should fight this battle," he ordered.

Ahab did as he asked and all the prophets said, "Oh yes! If you go into battle, you will surely win. The Lord will defeat your enemies for you!"

But Jehoshaphat did not trust these prophets. He thought they might not be telling the truth. Maybe they were just saying what they knew King Ahab wanted to hear. He said, "Isn't there a prophet who speaks truly for the Lord?"

"Well, yes there is," Ahab answered. "But I don't like him because he's always full of gloom and doom." Jehoshaphat said they should call the prophet anyway. This prophet's name was Micaiah, and like Elijah, he was a true man of God.

A messenger was sent to bring Micaiah to see the two kings. He told Micaiah, "Look, all the other prophets are telling the king that he will win. You had better say the same."

But Micaiah said, "The only thing I can do is to say whatever the Lord tells me."

When he arrived, King Ahab asked him, "Micaiah, should we fight or not?"

"Yes," he said. "Go ahead and attack. The Lord will help you win." Micaiah was just saying again what all the other prophets had said.

The king said, "How many times do I have to tell you that I want you to speak the truth from the Lord?"

"All right," Micaiah said. "I saw all Israel scattered on the hills like sheep without a shepherd. The Lord said, 'These people have no leader. Let them go home in peace.' "

The king of Israel said to Jehoshaphat, "See, didn't I tell you that he never prophesies anything good for me, but only bad?"

"I warn you," Micaiah continued, "the Lord has told me a lying spirit has been put in the mouths of all your prophets. You are heading for disaster."

Ahab became very angry. "Throw Micaiah into prison!" he said. Then the kings chose to ignore Micaiah's advice, and the kings went into battle against Syria.

Everything happened just at Micaiah had said. Before the battle, Ahab put on his armour and disguised himself. The Syrians were looking for him, as they had orders to kill Ahab on sight. But during the fighting an arrow hit Ahab, wounding him between his armour.

His men propped him up in the chariot so that no one would know he was dying, and the blood from his wound ran onto the floor. That evening he died. As the sun was setting, the armies of Israel and Judah lost the battle.

King Ahab was taken home and buried. His chariot was cleaned up, and the old prophecy of Elijah came true as the dogs licked up his blood from the chariot.

Some time later the prophecy given about Jezebel also came true. She was pushed from a balcony, and crashed to the ground. By the time the people came to bury her, dogs had already eaten her flesh.

The story of Jehoshaphat

1 Kings 22.41–43; 2 Chronicles 17.1–19; 19.1–20.37

King Ahab was killed during the battle against Syria, but God kept King Jehoshaphat safe from danger. He was like his father, King Asa. Both men were good kings because they tried to do whatever God wanted. They worshipped the one true God, and told the people that they should do the same.

King Jehoshaphat was king over Judah for twenty–five years. During that time he told the people who worshipped other gods to leave the land. He also sent teachers of God's law out into the villages. He wanted to make sure that everyone in his country would live according to God's laws. In that way the people would be cared for and have enough to eat, and justice and peace would fill the land.

Because he was a good king the Lord blessed Jehoshaphat. He had great riches and honour. Many of the enemy tribes around Judah didn't dare to make war with Jehoshaphat because they were afraid of the power of the Lord. Instead they gave him gifts of silver, sheep, and goats. Jehoshaphat built places to store food, and many forts, as well as making sure his army stayed strong.

While Jehoshaphat was king there was one group of enemies which did attack Judah. They came mainly from the countries of Ammon and Moab, and had a huge army. When Jehoshaphat heard that the enemy was close at hand, he told the people that they should stop eating and pray for help from God.

"O Lord," Jehoshaphat prayed, "you are powerful and mighty over all the nations. Will you judge our enemies? We cannot do anything without you. We do not know what to do, but we will wait for your answer."

Then the Lord spoke through a man in the crowd who worked in the temple. He said, "You must not be afraid to fight the battle tomorrow. The Lord will do that. Go out and face the enemy. The Lord is with you."

Jehoshaphat bowed to the ground in thanks, and all the people joined together in worship.

Early the next morning as they set out, Jehoshaphat stood and told them, "Listen to me, Judah and people of Jerusalem! Have faith in the Lord your God and you will be safe. Believe what his prophets tell you, and you will win!"

Jehoshaphat chose men to sing to the Lord and praise him as they went out. They marched ahead of the army, and as they began to sing for the Lord, God threw the enemy into panic. They fought each other instead of the people from Judah!

The men of Judah couldn't believe their eyes. There were dead bodies everywhere they looked. No one had escaped, and there was no enemy left. God had indeed fought their battle for them, and he had won!

So the people spent the next three days gathering all the clothing, jewellery and other valuables from the enemy. On the fourth day they praised the Lord and thanked him for everything. They named the valley where the battle had taken place, "The Valley of Praise."

The last days of Elijah

1 Kings 22.44–53; 2 Kings 1.1–17

While good King Jehoshaphat of Judah tried
to lead his people back to God, the son of
King Ahab of Israel turned out to be no better
than his evil father had been. When Ahab
died, his son Ahaziah became king. Ahaziah
worshipped Baal and not God, so the Lord
was not pleased with him.

Evil King Ahaziah reigned for only two
years. Near the end of that time he fell from
the balcony on the roof of his palace and
injured himself badly. "Go and ask the god
Baal if I will get better," he ordered his
messengers.

As these messengers were looking for the
priests of Baal, they met Elijah. Elijah asked
them, "The Lord wants to know why the king
looks for answers from a false god like Baal.
Why doesn't he ask the Lord God what will
happen? Go back and tell him he will die
from his injuries."

The messengers hurried back to the palace
and told the king what had happened. When
Ahaziah heard Elijah's message, he thought to
himself, "This Elijah caused trouble for my
father, King Ahab. Now he has bad news for
me, too. I know a way to make sure he
doesn't bother me any more."

"Go!" he ordered an officer. "Take fifty
men to capture Elijah."

The officer found Elijah sitting on top of a
hill. "Man of God," the officer said, "the king
orders you to come down." Elijah answered,
"If I am a man of God, may fire come down
and kill you and your men." At once fire
came down, and all fifty soldiers, together with
their officer, were killed.

Then the king sent another fifty men to
capture Elijah. But the same thing happened!
For a third time fifty more soldiers climbed up
Elijah's hill. Before he reached the top, the
officer of this group knelt down and begged
Elijah. "Please, have mercy on us, man of
God."

An angel of the Lord said to Elijah, "Go down with him and do not be afraid."

So Elijah followed the officer to the king's palace. There he asked the king the same thing he had asked the king's messengers. "Why didn't you ask God if you were going to get better? Why do you trust Baal more than the Lord? I will tell you why. It is because you are evil! Because you are so bad, you will never get well, but die."

This is exactly what happened.

The chariot of fire

2 Kings 2.1–12

Elijah had become an old man. All his life he had tried to lead the people back to God and away from the false god Baal. After he had said that evil King Ahaziah would die, Elijah knew it was almost time for the Lord to take him away.

Over the years Elisha had come to love Elijah, and they were like father and son. Elisha wanted to be as good a prophet as Elijah. Elijah gave the king and the people the Lord's message, and fought against evil and injustice in the land. He stood on God's side even when it might have cost him his life.

On their last day together, Elijah led Elisha to a place close to where Moses had died. Elijah was to be taken up to heaven in a whirlwind, so he told Elisha, "You stay here, while I go away."

But Elisha said, "As surely as the Lord lives and you live, I will not leave you." He knew they would not be together much longer.

Then some prophets who lived at Bethel went up to talk with Elisha about the old prophet. "Do you know that the Lord is going to take your teacher away today?" they asked.

"Yes, I do know," Elisha said. "But let's not talk about that now." Elisha loved Elijah very much and was sad that the Lord was going to take him away.

Once again Elijah asked Elisha to stay behind, but the younger man refused. "Why should I leave you now, when I have been at your side for so long?"

The two men went on. Then more of the Lord's prophets stopped them and said to Elisha, "Do you know your teacher will leave you today?"

"Yes," Elisha said. "I do know, but let's not talk about it." Then for a third time Elijah tried to send Elisha away, but he still wouldn't go.

Finally they reached the River Jordan. Elijah took off his cloak and folded it in half. He hit

the water with it, and the river divided in two
so that he and Elisha could cross to the other
side on dry ground. After they had walked
between the two walls of water Elijah said to
his young friend, "Tell me, what can I do for
you before I am taken away?"

Elisha said, "Pass on to me a double share
of the power the Lord has given you, just as if
I were your eldest son."

"Ah," Elijah sighed. "You ask for something
hard. But if you see me when I am taken
away from you, it will be given to you."

Then suddenly, while they were still walking
and talking together, a chariot of fire pulled by
horses of fire came between them. It blazed
like the sun, and the horses were aflame.
Then a huge whirlwind swept Elijah off the
ground, and he was taken up to heaven.

When Elisha saw it, he cried out, "My
father, my father! You were the true defender
of Israel, and now you are gone!"

Elisha shaded his eyes against the bright
sight before him, and was filled with

amazement. He never saw Elijah again.

Elisha was very sad about the loss of his friend, the great prophet Elijah. Yet he knew Elijah had been taken to heaven by the Lord, and that he had been chosen to become the next prophet. Over the years he had learnt from Elijah by serving him and being with him. He remembered the time that Elijah had first met him, and had thrown his cloak over Elisha's shoulders as he ploughed his father's field. Through Elisha God's work would go on, and God's power would be with him, just as it had been with Elijah.

Adventure Story Bible   Old Testament

Book 1   **In the Beginning**
             Genesis 1—22

Book 2   **Brother Against Brother**
             Genesis 23—41

Book 3   **The Years From Joseph to Moses**
             Genesis 41—50; Exodus 1—11

Book 4   **Moses Leads the People**
             Exodus 12—40; Deuteronomy 1; Leviticus

Book 5   **The Promised Land**
             Numbers; Deuteronomy; Joshua 1—4

Book 6   **Soldiers of the Lord**
             Joshua 5—end; Judges

Book 7   **Trusting God**
             Ruth; Job; 1 Samuel 1—2

Book 8   **Friends and Enemies**
1 Samuel 2—20

Book 9   **From Outlaw to King**
1 Samuel 21—31; Psalms 52, 59, 34, 142, 57, 23, 60;
2 Samuel 1—10; 1 Chronicles 10—20

Book 10   **King David's Reign**
2 Samuel 11—24; Psalms 32, 51, 3, 63, 18;
1 Kings 2; 1 Chronicles 11, 21—22; 2 Chronicles 3

Book 11   **True Wisdom**
1 Kings 1—4, 6—12; 1 Chronicles 22, 28—end; 2 Chronicles 1—11;
Psalm 72; Proverbs; Song of Solomon; Ecclesiastes

Book 12   **Working Wonders**
1 Kings 13—19, 21—22; 2 Kings 1—2, 9, 17, 22; 2 Chronicles 12—14, 17—20

Book 13   **Warning the People**
2 Kings 2, 4—9, 11, 13—14; 2 Chronicles 21—22, 25; 1 Kings 19; Isaiah 28—31; Amos

Book 14   **Prophets of God**
Hosea; Isaiah 1—9, 36—66; Micah; Joel; Jonah; 2 Kings 15—20; 2 Chronicles 26—32; Psalm 46

Book 15   **Heading for Disaster**
2 Kings 21—24; 2 Chronicles 33—36; Nahum; Zephaniah;
Jeremiah 1—2, 11—20, 26—28, 35—36, 45; Habakkuk; Psalm 73; Ezekiel 1—18

Book 16   **Homeless in Babylon**
2 Kings 24—25; 2 Chronicles 36; Jeremiah 24, 30—31, 37—40, 46—52; Ezekiel 24—32;
Isaiah 13—24, 40—43; Psalm 137; Lamentations; Obadiah; Daniel

Book 17   **Rebuilding Jerusalem**
Ezekiel 33—37, 40—48; Jeremiah 42—44; Isaiah 44—48; Ezra 1—4;
2 Chronicles 2, 36; Nehemiah 7; Esther

Book 18   **Hope for the Future**
Nehemiah 1—10, 12—13; Ezra 4—10; Haggai; Zechariah; Malachi; Isaiah 56—66

New Testament

Book 19   **The Early Years of Jesus**
Luke 1–5; Matthew 1–4, 14; Mark 1, 6; John 1–2

Book 20   **Healing Minds and Bodies**
John 2–5; Luke 4–7, 11, 12; Mark 1–3, 11; Matthew 5–10, 12, Isaiah 53

Book 21   **Following the Messiah**
Matthew 8–14; Luke 7–9, 11–13; Mark 3–6

Book 22   **Jesus Touches People**
Matthew 14–18; Mark 6–9; Luke 9; John 6

Book 23   **The Greatest Commandments**
Matthew 18; Luke 9–11, 13–15, 17; John 7–11

Book 24   **Believing the Truth**
Luke 15–20; Matthew 19–22, 26; Mark 10–12, 14; John 12

Book 25   **Jesus is Betrayed**
Matthew 22–26; Mark 12–14; Luke 20–22; John 12–18

Book 26   **Darkness Before the Dawn**
Matthew 26–27; Mark 14–15; Luke 22–23; John 18–19; Acts 1; Psalm 22

Book 27   **Jesus is Alive!**
Matthew 28; Mark 16; Luke 24; John 14–16, 20–end; Acts 1–11, 22, 26

Book 28   **The Early Church**
Acts 9–19; James; Galatians; 1 and 2 Thessalonians

Book 29   **The First Missionaries**
1 and 2 Corinthians; Acts 20–end; Romans; Ephesians; Philippians; Colossians

Book 30   **Good News for All Time**
*Philemon; 1 and 2 Peter; 1 and 2 Timothy; Titus; Hebrews;
Jude; 1, 2 and 3 John; Revelation*